ABIDE DEVOTIONAL

Forty Days to Abounding Freedom in Christ

John 15:5

Clay Meadows

ISBN 978-1-64492-228-6 (paperback)
ISBN 978-1-64492-229-3 (digital)

Christian Faith Publishing, Inc.
832 Park Avenue
Meadville, PA 16335
www.christianfaithpublishing.com

Printed in the United States of America

INTRODUCTION

Since the dawn of America, the culture of our country has become very different from when it began. Technology has had a significant impact on how we think and how we relate to one another. Technology has brought not just positives into our culture but negatives as well. For instance, we have become a culture of people who don't know how to wait on anything. We are used to instant results with the help of Google search and high-speed internet. Cell phones have become another appendage to our bodies. We carry them with us everywhere we go. Lost today is the art of unplugging and finding alone time with God. If something is difficult and takes time, we choose to move on to something new. It seems we have become a people who have to be constantly entertained in order to stay engaged. Even in church.

The unfortunate result has become more susceptible to bondage. Things such as social media which includes apps like Snapchat, Instagram, and more are dominating how we relate to our culture around us. Along with that has come bondage; bondage to our desire to present a false image of ourselves to the world. This leads to all kinds of addictions and oppression, particularly, the addiction of approval from others. Young adults especially don't know where to look to find peace or meaning in life. They work tirelessly on trying to find themselves by attempting to fulfill all their desires. We adults are no better sometimes. Often, we find our meaning in our children, jobs, or social status. When those things fail us, we lose our bearings because these things have become our idols. They have become our very reason for living.

The very things we love so much have become the source of our destruction, unless we can return to the source of our meaning and life, Jesus Christ. He is the only one worthy of our worship. This devotional is an attempt to return to our Creator and learn to lean and depend on Him for everything. Jesus is the source of our strength, our joy, our hope, our rest, and our salvation. We can't even obey Him with the right motives unless we continually commune with His Spirit. Christ Himself said in John 15: 5, "I am the vine; you are the branches. Whoever abides in me and I in him, he it is that bears much fruit, for apart from me you can do nothing."

When we are not connected to the vine, we are trying to live out of our own strength which leads to miserable failure. When we fail, we are emotionally defeated. When we feel defeated, we look to things in this world to fill the hurt and emptiness in our souls. Fear begins to dominate our thoughts and in turn will dictate our decisions. Only when we learn to abide in the vine, Jesus Christ, will we finally break free from the bondage of sin and fear. We must learn what it means to abide in Christ if we ever want to live in abounding freedom.

ACKNOWLEDGMENTS

The motivation for this devotional stems from a dear friend of mine, Denise Gray. In December of 2017, she revealed to her coworkers at First Assembly Christian School that she was diagnosed with lung cancer. She told us, the doctor informed her she had several tumors and that the prognosis was not good. Denise Gray happens to be one of the godliest people I have ever had the privilege to know. She is the kind of person when you meet her, you feel as if you have met Jesus Himself. She has so much love for everyone around her. Denise is also the kind of person that never has anything negative to say about other people. And when she says she will pray for you, you know she means it. So to find out she had such an aggressive cancer hit everyone that knows her very hard. At First Assembly Christian School, where I teach, morale took a severe drop, so I decided to begin writing a devotional to send to our faculty, staff, and administration with the hope that it would lift spirits and inspire prayer for Denise Gray and each other.

After several devotions were sent over a period of a few weeks, I felt the Lord put a desire in my heart to write about this subject of abiding in Christ. I realized that so much of our outlook in life is dependent on learning to abide in Him. Along with abiding in Christ, which is the foundation, I realized that we need to take steps to help us achieve this, such as the digestion of God's Word and the practice of prayer. When we learn to practice these two vital steps, they will lead to times of personal and social revival, which will also help us learn to abide in times of suffering. If we can learn to abide during times of tribulation, then, we will discover how to abide in hope, rest, and love. It is my utmost desire and goal that this devotional will bring honor and glory to our Lord Jesus Christ and will hopefully help us break free from the very things that enslave us.

ABIDE IN CHRIST

> I am the vine; you are the branches. If you
> remain in me and I in you, you will bear much
> fruit; apart from me you can do nothing.
> —John 15:5

Often in life, we get caught up in striving furiously to learn how to be better Christians who "bear much fruit." We read the latest books on how to become more spiritual or mature and, in turn, make plans to apply them to our daily lives, just to find out that it is exhausting. We often end up being burnt out from the endless effort we put into becoming what we believe to be more spiritual. Not that reading Christian books is wrong. It is a healthy habit which helps produce wisdom in our lives. But in order to "bear much fruit," what we need most is to be connected to the vine.

We must remember that the branch cannot make itself produce fruit. That is the job of the vine. The branch doesn't have to work in order to achieve this goal. In order to achieve this goal, we must immerse ourselves in the *Word that became flesh*. Rooting ourselves to the source will ensure that fruit will grow in us and overflow out of us. When this happens, the world will look at the true church and wonder how we can endure such trials, temptations, or setbacks and still have love, joy, peace, patience, kindness, goodness, faithfulness, gentleness, and self-control without being burnt out.

"Abide in Jesus, the sinless One—which means, give up all of self and its life, and dwell in God's will and rest in His strength. This is what brings the power that does not commit sin" (Andrew Murray).

TASTE AND SEE

Taste and see that the Lord is good.

—Psalm 34:8

John Piper said, "God is most glorified in us, when we are most satisfied in Him." For many, God appears as a distant judge who critiques everything we do. In their minds, God is quick to judge and harsh in His judgement. They believe the only way to gain the Lord's favor is by performing good deeds and keeping the law litigiously. What they have failed to see is that God is a loving Father who desires to commune with us. God wants us to intimately enjoy Him and find our ultimate satisfaction in Him. I was once told by a former professor of mine, "There is nothing you can do to earn God's favor, as a Christian you already have it." Christ has earned our favor for us with the Father. Seek the Lord today with all your heart, not for what He can do for you, but for Himself alone. God Himself is the gift.

"Our hearts are restless until they can find rest in you" (Augustine, Confessions).

THE UNQUENCHABLE THIRST OF THE SOUL

> Jesus answered her, "If you knew the gift
> of God and who it is that asks you for a
> drink, you would have asked him, and he
> would have given you living water."
>
> —John 4:10

Of all the encounters that Jesus had during His ministry on earth, this was perhaps one of the most revealing stories of our desperate thirst for God. Jesus intentionally seeks out the Samaritan woman and, in turn, teaches us a foundationally invaluable lesson to the Christian faith.

After his initial request for water and the claim that He has living water, Jesus gets to the heart of the matter by revealing that the Samaritan woman had been married five times and was now living with a man who was not her husband. Jesus was revealing to her the truth that the only thing that will quench the thirst of the soul in this life is *Himself, the living water.* The mistake she made is thinking that a man could fulfill those deep longings of the soul; a belief that if she finds the just the right husband life will be perfect. No one and nothing can ever fill the void that exists in our souls. Do you look to Jesus today to be your living water or something else?

"The essence of faith is being satisfied with all that God is for us in Jesus" (John Piper).

THE FREEDOM OF SECOND PLACE

Therefore, this joy of mine is now complete.
He must increase, but I must decrease.
—John 3:30

As a result of our fallen humanity, one of the many things we struggle with is the desire to be recognized and applauded for our achievements. Let's be honest, this affects those at the bottom of the totem pole all the way to the top. It's not a gender problem or an ethnic problem. It is a human problem. We all want to be appreciated for what we accomplish.

Part of what it means to abide in Christ (John 15) is to lose yourself in Him and recognize that any good work that comes from you is not really from you but is ultimately achieved by the Spirit of God. If anyone had a right to boast in Jesus's day, besides Jesus Himself, it was John the Baptist. Yet when his ministry is being disrupted by that of Jesus's, he is joyful. He knew that for humanity to have a chance, it needed Jesus more than him. This goes back to the old catechisms when it answers the question, "What is the chief end of man?" The answer given by the Westminster Shorter Catechism is, "Man's chief end is to glorify God and to enjoy him forever." John the Baptist lived this truth. Perhaps, this is why Jesus said, "Truly, I tell you, among those born of women, there has not risen anyone greater than John the Baptist."

Let us remember to daily take ourselves off the throne of our hearts and allow God to have His rightful place.

"I'd rather have Jesus than worldly applause, I'd rather be faithful to his dear cause" (Rhea F. Miller and George Beverly Shea).

REFLECTING THE GLORY OF GOD

When Moses came down from Mount Sinai
with the two tablets of the covenant law in
his hands, he was not aware that his face was
radiant because he had spoken with the Lord.
—Exodus 34:29

One major benefit of abiding with Christ is the impact it has on those around us. The more time we spend with Christ, the more we will look like Him. It is common knowledge that we become like the ones we spend the most time with. Is that not true of spending time with Jesus?

Much like how Moses reflected the glory of God, we can reflect the love of Christ onto the people in our environment. Just imagine, as a result of becoming more intimate in our walk with Jesus, people who pass by us can sense a difference without us even saying a word. The aroma of Christ in us will cause others in our path to ask us what is so different about ourselves. They will feel either peace or conviction just by being near us. In order to achieve this, we must learn who we were created to be, and we cannot know who we are until we begin to know Christ better. Who can better help one learn who they are and what they are designed for than the One who designed them. Let us abide in Christ today so that we can know ourselves and reflect the glory of God in our daily life.

"It is only into the thirst of an empty soul that the streams of living waters flow. Ever thirsting is the secret to never thirsting" (Andrew Murray).

ABIDE IN THE WORD

Keep this Book of the Law always on your
lips; meditate on it day and night, so that you
may be careful to do everything written in it.
Then you will be prosperous and successful.
—Joshua 1:8

In our fast-paced culture, it is easy to neglect the reading of God's Holy Word. The busyness may come in the form of work, home, career, personal hobbies, or even in service of others. Distraction from God's Word doesn't always come in the form of something obviously sinful. But at the same time, the Word of God is our nourishment, our source of strength, wisdom, and hope.

Jesus set a perfect example for us in the wilderness on how the Word of God will cause us to be "*prosperous and successful.*" When the devil himself tempted Jesus, He only responded with scripture. Jesus said something profound that we all need to capture and embody in our own lives. He said, "*Man shall not live by bread alone, but by every word that comes from the mouth of God.*" By abiding in God's Word, we will find every rich treasure we will ever need. We will have the power to stand firm when trials or temptations come our way. We will have an answer when someone asks us to give an account for our faith. Let us never forget that the only thing the Holy Spirit can work within you is the Holy Word of God.

"A Bible that's falling apart usually belongs to someone who isn't" (Charles Spurgeon).

THE WORD RENDERS
AND RESTORES

> When the king heard the words of the Book
> of the law, he tore his robes. He gave the
> orders... "Go and inquire of the Lord for me
> and for the people and for all Judah what is
> written in this book that has been found."
> —2 Kings 22: 11–13

When King Josiah was still young, he gave orders to have the temple rebuilt, and in the process, Hilkiah found the Book of the law. After listening to the reading of the law, Josiah tore his robe in agony of Judah's sin of idolatry. King Josiah, a good man already, became acutely aware of the idol worship currently going on in the land and becomes grieved by it.

The Word of God pierced his soul rendering it and at the same time restored it as well. The message for the Judah was one of anger from the Lord and was revealed through the prophet Huldah that God would bring about "disaster." Yet for Josiah, because of his humility stirred by God's Word, the Lord's message for him was one of grace. The message for Josiah was that while he lived, the land would not see disaster. Even though Josiah knew that God's judgment would come, because of the Lord's Word and the impact it had on him, he continued to purge the country of idol worship and persuade the people to serve the One and only true God. The Word of God is anointed and life-giving. It is time for us to pick it up, read and digest it, and let it do its work in and through us.

"A Bible that's falling apart usually belongs to someone who isn't" (Charles Spurgeon).

CONTINUE IN THE WORD

So Jesus was saying to those Jews who had
believed Him, "If you continue in My word,
then you are truly disciples of Mine."
—John 8:31

Imagine, for a moment, that a young lady receives a letter from a man she loves. Do you think for a second that she will put the note down and wait several weeks before she even opens the letter? Of course not! This letter came from someone she loves and adores. She would open it right away to see what he wrote to her. This is how you can tell if a woman really loves the man. She'll jump at the chance to read his letter, instead of casually throwing it down to save it for another day when she has more time?

In the same way, one can tell who truly is in love with the Lord. Jesus Himself said, "If you continue in My word, then you are truly disciples of Mine." The Word of God is not something to be taken lightly. It is a letter from the Almighty Creator of the universe who loves us dearly. How can we not desire to read and devour the Holy Word of God? Let us continue daily in the Word so that we it will be said of us that we "are truly disciples" of Jesus Christ.

"Oh, give me that book! At any price give me the book of God. Let me be a man of one book" (John Wesley).

MEDITATE ON THE WORD

But his delight is in the law of the LORD, and
in His law he meditates day and night.
—Psalm 1:2

Most of the time, when the word meditation is mentioned in Christian circles, it brings images of eastern religions such as Buddhism or Hinduism. There is a strong and common reaction among evangelicals that meditation is a pagan practice. Meditating on God's Word is not the same thing that eastern religions are doing though. Christian meditation is not sitting in a yoga position emptying your mind. It is a different thing altogether. Mediating on the Word means to not just read the Bible but to study it as well. We are to pore over and digest the word as if it were our food. Jesus Himself said that "man shall not live by bread alone, but by every word that comes from the mouth of God."

As Christians, it is important to think daily of God's Word, what it means, and how we apply it to our lives. We are never called to empty our minds in order to find peace or balance. Second Timothy 2:15 says, "Do your best to present yourself to God as one approved, a worker who has no need to be ashamed, rightly handling the word of truth."

"The very practice of reading the Bible will have a purifying effect upon your mind and heart. Let nothing take the place of this daily exercise" (Billy Graham).

Streams of Water

He will be like a tree firmly planted by
streams of water, which yields its fruit
in its season and its leaf does not wither;
and whatever he does, he prospers.
—Psalm 1:3

When our "delight is in the law of the *lord*" and we begin to mediate on His word, we will be connected to everlasting streams of water. Much like a tree, these waters of scripture will supply us with the nourishment that we need to flourish in life. The fruits of the Spirit will begin to take root in our hearts and will bloom in our actions.

My father once told me that if you store the Word of God in your heart, the Holy Spirit will bring it to your mind whenever you need it. When life gets tough and we're faced with what appears to be hopeless circumstances, we certainly won't be able to trust our feelings. That's when the Spirit uses the Word of God in you to bring about times of refreshing. Most encouraging, everything we do will prosper. This is God's definition of prospering, not the world's. It doesn't mean that we will get every material thing we desire or every promotion we work for. What it does means is that we will be successful in furthering the Kingdom of God. That is real prosperity.

"If you would follow on to know the Lord, come at once to the open Bible expecting it to speak to you. Do not come with the notion that it is a thing which you may push around at your convenience. It is more than a thing; it is a voice, a word, the very Word of the living God" (A.W. Tozer).

ABIDE IN PRAYER

And pray in the Spirit on all occasions
with all kinds of prayers and request. With
this in mind, be alert and always keep
on praying for all the Lord's people."

Much like the reading of Scripture, our prayer lives have a tendency to be neglected. Our fast-paced culture is too busy to let us stop and take a breath. Even the church can get so caught up in working for the Lord that they forget to be with Him. Not that working for the Lord is a bad thing, but it should not cause us to skip our prayer time with the One we love most. Our time spent in prayer will only enhance the work that we do for the Lord.

Charles Finney, a man known for spending hours at a time in prayer, understood this truth better than most people. At the time of his salvation, he spent hours in the woods and said, "I will give my heart to God, or I never will come down from there." This is the same man who walked into a cotton mill, never uttered a word, and people began to tremble at the presence of the Holy Spirit. The story goes that the boss, who was not a Christian, came out of his office and said, "Stop the mill, and let the people attend to religion. For it is more important that our souls should be saved than that this factory run." Prayer is powerful and effective and should never be put on the backburner for anything, including what we would consider the "good things."

"Unless I had the Spirit of prayer, I could do nothing" (Charles Finney).

Pray in the Morning

O Lord, in the morning, you hear
my voice; in the morning I prepare a sacrifice for you and watch.
—Psalm 5:3

Most, if not everyone, has had that dream when you are sitting in your college class and you find out its exam day and you haven't studied. The feeling of terror begins to overwhelm us, and we think to ourselves, *How could I have let this happen?* No one likes to feel unprepared for something important in their lives, for instance, an exam or presentation. If we dread being unprepared for little things such as this, then why do we not hold our upcoming day with the same value; should we not prepare for our day as much as anything else?

Prayer in the early morning is the best way to get ready for the unknown that you will face. In Mark 1:35, it says, "And rising very early in the morning, while it was still dark, he departed and went out to a desolate place, and there he prayed." Jesus understood the value of rising before the sun and speaking to His Father. If it's good enough for Jesus, it should be good enough for us. Let us begin a new routine of bathing our day in prayers of adoration, praise, and supplication to our heavenly Father, who desires to hear from us.

"Prayer is our most formidable weapon, the thing which makes all else we do efficient" (E.M. Bounds).

PRAY WITHOUT CEASING

Rejoice always, pray without ceasing, give
thanks in all circumstances; for this is the
will of God in Christ Jesus for you.
—1 Thessalonians 5:16–18

Prayer without ceasing is the very definition of abiding in Christ. Prayer without ceasing doesn't mean that you must be verbally praying all day long. What it means is we are to be mindful of His constant presence throughout our day. We should be asking Jesus for wisdom in our daily decisions, strength in our weaknesses, and peace in our troubles. We should also take prayer without ceasing to mean that we are in fellowship with Christ all throughout the day. We should see it as we would see a friend walking with us because that's exactly what it is. We have a friend who is always with us wherever we go. His omnipresence will never let us be away from Him.

Prayer is not a set of religious phrases that sound spiritual; it is talking and listening to God. It's that simple. We make it more difficult than it should be. Remember, today, you can talk to the Almighty God whenever you like. He is always available and eager to be in fellowship with you.

"God's command to pray without ceasing is founded on the necessity we have of His grace to preserve the life of God in the soul, which can no more subsist one moment without it, than the body can without air" (John Wesley).

Expectant Prayer

Therefore, I tell you, whatever you
ask in prayer, believe that you have
received it, and it will be yours.
—Mark 11:24

For many Christians, Mark 11:24 is where the rubber meets the road. We read this verse and we try to explain how it doesn't mean what it sounds like. We say we can't always have what we want in life. That's true, we can't get everything we want, but what we've also done is create a sense of doubt about trusting God's Word. Remember, God is our Heavenly Father "who is able to do far more abundantly than all that we ask or think." If we ask for more faith or wisdom, do we not think that He will open up heaven itself and pour out a blessing on us? God is eager to answer our prayers. Our problem, according to James 4:3, is we "ask and do not receive, because you ask wrongly, to spend it on your passions." The other problem that James said we have is that we ask with doubt in our hearts. He said in chapter 1:6–7, "*But let him ask in faith, with no doubting, for the one who doubts is like a wave of the sea that is driven and tossed by the wind. For that person must not suppose that he will receive anything from the Lord.*" If it is victory we need in our lives, let us believe without a doubt that God will provide. If it is anything that would bring honor to God, then let us trust in the character of God the way Abraham did. Let us expect God to live up to His character, because He can do no less.

"Without faith it is impossible to please Him" (Hebrews 11:6).

Prayer of Adoration

Because your love is better than life, my lips
will glorify you. I will praise you as long as I
live, and in your name, I will lift up hands.
—Psalm 63:3-4

One of the greatest benefits of prayer is that when we begin to become more intimate with the Lord, we will inherently develop an overwhelming sense of adoration for Him. This attitude of worship will become as natural as breathing the more God reveals Himself to us. David, a man after God's own heart, is a sterling example of what it looks like to adore God. In 2 Samuel 24:24, after Araunah offered some land for David to offer God a sacrifice, David replied, "No, but I will buy it from you for a price. I will not offer burnt offerings to the LORD my God that cost me nothing."

You can say a lot of things about David, whether it be that he was an adulterer, a murderer, or a terrible father, but one thing you can't say about King David was that he didn't love God. That man adored God with all of his heart. His many psalms reveal his heart for his Heavenly Father. While there is always a place for supplications, confessions, and intercessions in prayer, the highest form of prayer that we can achieve is adoration for our Creator.

"My aim each day is to adore God more than anything else" (A.W. Tozer).

ABIDE IN THE FIRE

Suddenly, a sound like the blowing of a violent wind came from heaven and filled the whole house where they were sitting. They saw what seemed to be tongues of fire that separated and came to rest on each of them.
—Acts 2:2-3

When a heart with an unquenchable desire sets out on a relentless journey to find God, the result will be an all-consuming fire. Few knew this better than the followers of Jesus in the upper room. It was ten days in between the ascension of Jesus and the day of Pentecost. They spent those ten days in prayer, waiting for the Helper that Jesus promised them.

Many Christians today say they want to see revival in the land, but few are willing to pay the cost to get it. In order to receive an all-consuming fire from the Lord which will have ripple effects on the culture around us, you must pursue the Lord with fervor and even wait upon Him as long as necessary. As a result of their faithful pursuit and patience, the apostles were able to turn the world upside down. How bad do we want to see the fire of God move? Are we willing to give what is necessary to make it happen?

"The only reason we don't have revival is because we are willing to live without it" (Leonard Ravenhill).

A Brand Plucked
from the Fire

> As he neared Damascus on his journey, sud-
> denly, a light from heaven flashed around him.
> He fell to the ground and heard a voice say to
> him, "Saul, Saul, why do you persecute me?"
> —Acts 9:3-4

When he was only five years of age, John Wesley narrowly escaped what could have been a very tragic home fire. It was said that John's father couldn't get to his son after several attempts to save him, so people began to pray. Then, John walked to a window where a neighbor was able to rescue him just before the floor underneath him gave way. Later in Wesley's life, after his return from America, he had a life altering experience on a street called Aldersgate. He heard a rendering of Luther's commentary on the book of Romans and was never the same. It was the message regarding faith in Christ alone for salvation that caused him to say, "I felt my heart strangely warmed." This "brand plucked from the fire" became enflamed with the fire of God.

What followed after was a revival the world would never forget. Nearly two thousand years ago, a young man named Saul was rescued from the fires of hell on the road to Damascus by Christ Himself. Not only was he empowered with the fire of God, he set the world ablaze with the power of the Gospel. Let our hearts today meditate on the truth that we receive grace through faith in Christ alone. Then let us pick up the torch that has been passed down to us and bring fire back to our world.

"I set myself on fire, and people come to watch me burn" (John Wesley).

THE COST

For whoever would save his life will lose it, but
whoever loses his life for my sake will find it.
—Matthew 16:25

When Polycarp of Smyrna, an early church father, was eighty-six years old, he was arrested by the Roman government for his faith in Christ. As a result of denying the request of the proconsul, Polycarp was then sentenced to be burned at the stake. The witnesses who were believers said they heard a voice shout, "Be strong, Polycarp, and play the man." The story has it that when the wood was lit, the fire formed an arch around Polycarp, and the witnesses said, "He looked not like flesh that is burnt, but like bread that is baked… And we smelt a sweet scent, like frankincense or some precious spices."

When we honor God and crucify ourselves daily so that His precious Son may live through us, when the fires comes, instead of burning our flesh, it will reveal the Spirit within us and release a sweet aroma.

"Every man dies, not every man really lives" (Braveheart).

FAITH REVEALED BY FIRE

These have come so that the proven gen-
uineness of your faith—of greater worth
than gold, which perishes even though
refined by fire—may result in praise, glory
and honor when Jesus Christ is revealed.
—1 Peter 1:7

Job's faith was proven genuine when tested by the fires unleashed on him by the devil. His word, "Even though you slay me, I will still trust you," sends a resounding message that he loved God, even if he got nothing out of it. There is another Job in the New Testament, Jesus Christ. Job may have been blameless, but Christ was sinless. Jesus never did anything deserving of punishment, He always obeyed His Father, and He still got crushed for our iniquity. In the Garden of Gethsemane, when His "soul was sorrowful to the point of death", Jesus uttered the words, "Not my will, but Thy will be done." Will we love God and trust Him even if it costs us our reputations, our bank accounts, our friends, and maybe even our desires? The fire will reveal what our hearts love most in this life. Let it be that, of all the things the world can say about us, the one thing it can never say is that we "don't love God."

"Love the Lord your God with all your heart and with all your soul and with all your mind" (Matthew 22:37).

UNBOUND

And these three men, Shadrach, Meshach,
and Abednego, fell *bound* into the burning fiery furnace... But I see four men
unbound, walking in the midst of the fire,
and they are not hurt; and the appearance
of the fourth is like a son of the gods.
—Daniel 3:23, 25

One thing we fail to see when the fires come in our lives is that if we are in Christ, the only thing it will do is set us free from our restraints. Paul was correct when he said, "No weapon formed against us shall prosper." So often when the trial comes, we focus on asking God to get us out and deliver us from the situation. When, in actuality, we should be asking God to burn off anything that has held us back from forming a more intimate relationship with Him. And when the restraints are burned off, we are free to glorify God and further His kingdom. Every attempt from the enemy on a child of God will ultimately backfire on him. God gives the devil just enough rope for him to hang himself. To summarize Martin Luther, the devil is still God's devil.

"So if the Son sets you free, you will be free indeed" (John 8:36).

ABIDE IN SUFFERING

Count it all joy, my brothers, when you meet
trials of various kinds, for you know that the
testing of your faith produces steadfastness. And
let steadfastness have its full effect, that you may
be perfect and complete, lacking in nothing.
—James 1:2–4

One of the hardest lessons in life to learn is waiting in the midst of suffering. No one likes it, and almost all resist it initially. The riches that come from learning to abide in suffering though are invaluable. As James said, "Your faith produces steadfastness," and steadfastness will be necessary if you want to finish strong in the short time that we're given in this life.

Few knew suffering better than the Apostle Paul. This was a man who was beaten, flogged, stoned, lost at sea, and imprisoned for a significant amount of time. And Paul still was able to say that He had learned the secret of being content. By learning to abide in suffering, Paul became a difficult target for the enemy. Nothing could seemingly shake the man. He could even boast in his own weakness. The secret of learning to abide in suffering is complete surrender to God and complete trust in His goodness. If we can get to that place where we surrender and trust completely, we will be like the house built on the rock that stands strong even in the most violent of storms.

"While other worldviews lead us to sit in the midst of life's joys, foreseeing the coming sorrows, Christianity empowers its people to sit in the midst of this world's sorrows, tasting the coming joy" (Tim Keller).

Broken and Spilled Out (Part 1)

Even if I am to be poured out as a drink
offering upon the sacrificial offering of your
faith, I am glad and rejoice with you all.

Often in life, we feel as if we've been broken and poured out for others. The feelings of brokenness may come as the result of ungratefulness from those we serve, being lowered so others can be lifted up, or being ridiculed undeservingly. The truth is we are never more like Christ when we are being broken and spilled out by God for His glory and the benefit of others. For the glory of the Father, the redemption of mankind, and the destruction of death itself, Christ's body was broken for us and His blood spilled out. The only way for us as Christians to survive the breaking process is to search our hearts and make sure that everything we do in life is done unto the Lord. The next time we feel broken and spilled out, let us rejoice and be like Peter and John and thank God for being worthy to suffer shame for His name.

"Broken and spilled out and poured at Your feet in sweet abandon, let me be spilled out and used up for Thee" (Steve Green).

BROKEN AND SPILLED OUT (PART 2)

> Mary, therefore, took a pound of expen-
> sive ointment made from pure nard and
> anointed the feet of Jesus and wiped his
> feet with her hair. The house was filled
> with the fragrance of the perfume.

I once heard Emerson Eggriches, author of *Love and Respect*, give an analogy about how stress and pressure reveal what is inside of our hearts. In his *Love and Respect* conference, he said that if he were to step on a skunk, an awful smell would obviously be released. He mentioned that he did not cause the skunk to smell like that but that the pressure he put on it revealed what was on the inside. In contrast, he said that if he stepped on a rose, the pressure would release a pleasant aroma.

This sobering truth is what happens to us when we encounter trials in our life. The trials reveal the character inside of us. If the aroma that comes from us is not what we would like it to be, then consider the trial a gift of humility. On the other hand, for the one who is surrendered to God in love, when they are broken and spilled out, the sweet aroma of Christ's Spirit will be released on those around you and will cause them to seek after the Lord. Mother Teresa said, "Some people come in our life as blessings. Some come in your life as lessons." Which one will you be today?

"Above all else, guard your heart, for everything you do flows from it" (Proverbs 4:23).

A SONG OF REASSURANCE
IN THE NIGHT

> But none says, "Where is God my Maker,
> who gives songs in the night, who teaches us
> more than the beasts of the earth and makes
> us wiser than the birds of the heavens?"

Just recently, I had an unexpected encounter with the Lord. On February 13, 2018, I left my house around 6:30 p.m. to put gas in my Tahoe. Leading up to this night, life had been particularly dark for my family and had intensified in the last three weeks or so. While I was trying to enjoy one of the few quiet moments I receive throughout the day, I heard a song bird singing not too far above me. At first, I didn't think anything of it, but as I continued to pump gas, the bird just seems to linger above me singing beautifully. Then, the thought crossed my mind, *Is that You, Lord? Are You giving me a song in the night?*

After I got home, I didn't think about it until the next morning when I read from Oswald Chambers devotional *My Utmost for His Highest.* The devotional was about hearing, but it was the second sentence that caught my attention. It read, "Song birds are taught to sing in the dark, and God puts us into 'the shadow of His hand' until we learn to hear Him." All I could do in that moment was praise Him. The only thing that mattered in that moment was that the Creator of heaven and Earth cared enough about me to give me a song of reassurance in the night.

If you are going through your own darkness right now, just know that the Lord has not forgotten you. His gentle reassurance is more than enough to see you through.

"He who dwells in the shelter of the Most High will abide in the shadow of the Almighty" (Psalm 91:1).

Faith Revealed by Fire Part 2

> These have come so that the proven gen-
> uineness of your faith—of greater worth
> than gold, which perishes even though
> refined by fire—may result in praise, glory,
> and honor when Jesus Christ is revealed.
> —1 Peter 1:7

When Peter wrote this letter, he was addressing a group of Christians suffering at the hands of Roman persecution under Nero. Peter encourages his readers to be patient in suffering and to put their hope in Christ, who is their living hope. This passage of Scripture has always made me think of Job. Much like Job's story, we can ascertain that our faith will be tested in this life. Our faith, like gold, will be tested by fire. Satan's goal was to get Job to curse God, and he took everything from him except his wife in order to accomplish that goal. While we know that Job received tenfold what he lost, the interesting thing about this story is that God never tells him about the conversation between Himself and Lucifer. Job never gets an explanation to why. Yet Job could still say, "Though you slay me, I will trust you." The reason he could say that is because he learned to love God, even if he got nothing out of it. His gift was and is the Redeemer. The fire revealed in Job a selfless love for his Creator. Will our fire reveal the same result?

"Realize that God uses the fires of life to purify your faith, to shape you into Christ's image, and to cause you to love Him...even more" (Elizabeth George)!

ABIDE IN HOPE

"For I know the plans I have for you," declares
the Lord, "plans to prosper you and not to harm
you, plans to give you hope and a future."
—Jeremiah 29:11

Behind love, hope may be the most powerful tool God has given us through His Holy Spirit. It gives us the ability to withstand anything this life will throw at us. Pastor Tom Lindberg of First Assembly Memphis used to say that "we can live at most a month without food, a few days without water, and a few minutes without oxygen. But we can't live even a second without hope."

In the book *Man's Search for Meaning*, Victor Frankl wrote about a man, who was in the concentration camp with him, who had a dream that the war would end on March 30. When the man realized on the 29 that the war was not even close to an end, he became very sick and died on March 31. Frankl wrote regarding this man, "The prisoner who lost faith in the future—his future—was doomed. With his loss of belief in the future, he also lost his spiritual hold; he let himself decline and became subject to mental and physical decay." As Christians, we have our hope anchored in Christ and His promises to us through His Word. Take hold today and abide in His promise "to give you hope and a future."

"And now, O Lord, for what do I wait? My hope is in you" (Psalm 39:7).

A LIVING HOPE

According to his great mercy, he has caused
us to be born again to a living hope through
the resurrection of Jesus Christ from the dead,
to an inheritance that is imperishable, unde-
filed, and unfading, kept in heaven for you.
—1 Peter 1:3–4

Tom Hanks in *Cast Away* gives an encouraging picture of a living hope. In one of the final scenes, Tom Hanks reveals to his friend what it was like on being stranded on an island for four years with only the thought of the woman he loved to keep him going. He then confessed about his failed plan for a suicide attempt. He said that when he realized he couldn't even kill himself the way he wanted to, the feeling that came over him was like a warm blanket. Hanks said, "I knew what I had to do. I had to keep breathing, because tomorrow the sun would rise." Four years later, the tide provided him a sail which helped him get past the tide and led to his rescue. The most heartbreaking part of the scene was when he told his friend that even though he's back home, he's lost the woman he loved all over again. Helen Hunt's character, believing Hanks was dead, married and had children. Hanks ends the scene with this powerful response, "I've lost her all over again, but I know what I have to do. I have to keep breathing, because tomorrow the sun will rise. Who knows what the tide will bring."

Tom Hank's character's hope is anchored in something higher than himself. While his hope may not be in God, we, as Christians, have a solid assurance: "All things turn out for good to those that love the Lord." When we go through our dark times, we can all rest assured that tomorrow, the sun will rise. Who knows what God will bring?

"Weeping may tarry for the night, but joy comes with the morning" (Psalm 30:5).

AN ETERNAL HOPE

What no eye has seen, nor ear heard, nor
the heart of man imagined, what God
has prepared for those who love Him.

At times, our lives can be so consumed with spiritual warfare that our future appears bleaker than it actually is. It is easy, while in the midst of suffering, to lose sight of hope. In the *Lord of the Rings*, just before one of the last battles, a hobbit named Pippin said to the wizard, Gandalf, "I didn't think it would end this way."

Gandalf: End? No, the journey doesn't end here. Death is just another path, one that we all must take. The grey rain-curtain of this world rolls back, and all turns to silver glass, and then you see it.

Pippin: See what?

Gandalf: White shores, and beyond, a far green country under a swift sunrise.

Pippin: Well, that isn't so bad.

Gandalf: No. No, it isn't.

Paul understood better than anyone what it meant to suffer. He also understood better than anyone what was waiting for those who love the Lord. Paul had been given a glimpse of heaven and was ordered by God to not tell anyone what he saw. No matter what trial or suffering we face in this life, someday, the veil will be pulled back, and we will see it. See what? *Jesus Christ.*

"Anticipating heaven doesn't eliminate pain, but it lessens it and puts it in perspective" (Randy Alcorn).

HEAVENLY PERSPECTIVE

And Elisha prayed, "Open his eyes, Lord, so that
he may see." Then the LORD opened the servant's eyes, and he looked and saw the hills full
of horses and chariots of fire all around Elisha.
—2 Kings 6:17

Try to imagine what it must have been like for Elisha's servant for just
a moment. He wakes up and goes outside his tent and sees that they
are surrounded by the enemy. That's an awful predicament to be in.
While I highly doubt any of us have woken up with our homes surrounded by people with swords and shields, we *have* had times in our
life when we were overwhelmed with fear and discouragement. And
whether we know it or not, we do have an enemy who never sleeps
and will stop at nothing in order to destroy us. Yet our defender is
strong and always ready. Also, don't forget, the devil only took one-
third of the angels which means there are two angels for every one
demon. And if that is not enough, our God, who is infinite and
omnipresent can, by Himself, surround all of our foes. Be encour-
aged and ask God to give you a heavenly perspective.

"A day may come when the courage of men fails, when we for-
sake our friends and break all bonds of fellowship, but it is not this
day" (Aragorn, *The Return of the King*).

HOPE LEADS TO ACTION

> She came up behind him and touched
> the fringe of his garment, and immedi-
> ately, her discharge of blood ceased.
> —Luke 8:44

In Luke 8, we see a woman who had been ill for twelve years. Verse 43 of chapter 8 says, "She had spent all her living on physicians." Imagine being oppressed by a sickness for twelve years, and the doctors can do nothing to cure the disease.

Many of us today can relate to having an illness that borders on being debilitating. That's why hope is so vital in a Christian's life. Hope is one of the most powerful weapons we have in our arsenal for the spiritual war we wake up to each day. Hope will always lead to action. Hope led this woman, who could have easily given up after suffering for so long, to fight her way through a busy crowd just so she could find healing through Jesus Christ. Hope, by itself, is not enough though. Our hope must be anchored in Christ alone for it to have results. By putting Christ as her object of hope, she was healed. Jesus said in verse 48, "Daughter, your *faith* has made you well; go in peace." Faith and hope are interwoven together. Hebrews 11:1 says, "Now faith is the substance of things *hoped* for, the evidence of things not seen." Let hope cause us to rise up and seek our Savior with a new fervor that will bring honor and glory to His Name.

"Hope means expectancy when things are otherwise hopeless" (G. K. Chesterton).

ABIDE IN REST

Come to me, all you who are weary and
burdened, and I will give you rest. Take
my yoke upon you and learn from me,
for I am gentle and humble in heart, and
you will find rest for your souls. For my
yoke is easy and my burden is light.
—Matthew 11:28–30

Finding real rest in our world today can be a difficult thing to do. The more we pursue it, the more evasive it seems to become. Why is it so hard to find rest for our souls? It is because we depend too much on the external things that God has given us for our source of rest. Jesus said, "I will give you rest." Learning to abide in rest is dependent on learning to abide in Christ. Without the foundation of Christ, rest will be impossible to come by.

George Whitefield once encountered a bout with oppression. It happened to him while spending time in the holiness club with John and Charles Wesley. He tried to fight the oppression with what could be called holy acts. He tithed more, served more, prayed more, etc. Nothing seemed to work, until one day, he came across the passage of scripture with Jesus on the Cross crying out, "I thirst." He said that he realized that after Jesus said those words, his suffering was not going to last much longer. He understood that Jesus was thirsty for more than just water. Jesus was thirsty for His Father in heaven. It was at this realization that Whitefield's oppression left immediately. This is what it means to *find rest for your souls.* Let our souls find its rest in the sweet presence of Christ alone.

"If you look at the world, you'll be distressed. If you look within, you'll be depressed. If you look at God, you'll be at rest" (Corrie Ten Boom).

The Gospel and Rest

See what great love the Father has lavished on us, that we should be called children of God! And that is what we are!
—1 John 3:1

Abiding in the Gospel is about realizing our worth and identities are not determined by our success or failures, others' opinions, our income, our social status, or anything else this world can offer us. Abiding in the Gospel is about finding our worth and identity in the Gospel message itself. The Gospel tells us we are sinners who are desperately wicked, yet it also tells us we are loved and adored to the point that *"the Father has lavished on us"* His *"great love."*

When we begin to own this truth in our lives, we will get to the point when our failures will no longer crush us; our mistakes will no longer define who we are. Because of Christ Jesus, we are now children of God. The Gospel will also keep us from arrogance. Even our successes in life will not define us, because we now understand that while I am loved, I cannot earn favor with my Father in heaven. Only Christ could do that. Only when we learn to abide in the Gospel will we ever find true freedom—freedom from looking to others or even ourselves for worth. From now on, we only find our worth in the one true God whose love endures forever.

"Then you will know the truth, and the truth will set you free" (John 8:32).

HE RESTORES MY SOUL

The Lord is my shepherd; I shall not want. He
makes me lie down in green pastures. He leads
me beside still waters. He restores my soul.
—Psalm 23:1–3

As a teacher, nine months out of the year for me can be very busy. I live and breathe by deadlines, for myself and for my students. With every passing year, this passage has taken on a life of its own in my walk with Christ. The words "He restores my soul," have become the very thing I long for most. Life can be very daunting and thankless at times. As Christians who work hard to further the kingdom of God, we desperately need the Lord to restore our souls.

Picture with me for a moment what these green pastures look like; a wide-open space with beautiful green grass with trees and mountains in the distance. Perhaps, a stream nearby for the still waters that Psalm 23 mentioned. There is no sound with the exception of the stream nearby. The air around is filled with the eclectic smells of nature. And best of all, imagine the presence of the Almighty filling the air with His sweet aroma. Believe it or not, we can find rest for our souls like this, even in the midst of troubled times. Often, people will run to massage parlors or the beach in order to find rest, but there is nothing in this world that can restore your soul other than God Himself.

"We imitate God by stopping our work and resting" (Peter Scazzero).

THE SHELTER AND THE SHADOW

> He who dwells in the shelter of the Most High
> will abide in the shadow of the Almighty.
> —Psalm 91:1

When reading the words of Psalm 91:1, one can't help but feel the presence of the one who inspired them—the Holy Spirit. These inspired words convey the strength and the majesty of God. How important is it for people who live in the center of persecution to know that the God they serve is omnipotent and omnipresent? For starters, there is nowhere we can go where God's presence does not dwell. Also, there is no force on earth that could remotely challenge His strength and might. This truth, when taken to heart and owned by the believer, will bring an unshakeable peace, because they will know that God is their shelter. With His shadow, God will create an environment of peace and rest in our souls. Notice that the environment of peace and rest that God will create is not necessarily external but rather internal.

Psalm 91:1 has been a haven of comfort and rest for many Christians throughout the centuries. It can be and has been the same for us today. The choice to rest is in our hands. No matter our foe, let us dwell "in the shelter of the Most High" so that we can "abide in the shadow of the Almighty."

"After creation, God said, 'It is finished,' and He rested. After redemption, Jesus said, "It is finished,' and we can rest" (Tim Keller).

You Alone, O Lord

In peace, I will both lie down and sleep; for
you alone, O Lord, make me dwell in safety.
—Psalm 4:8

"You alone, O Lord" is not just a phrase but an outlook on life. It is a perspective of humility with the knowledge that it is only by the grace of God that we have air in our lungs. Even more, there is nothing of any substance that we can do in this life without the help of our Lord Jesus Christ. This is encouraging truth for us because this truth pertains to our sleep as well. Believe or not, God takes a personal interest in our sleep. Often, people will say that they can't get to sleep early or rest well, because they have too much on their minds. What happens is we stress ourselves trying to figure out how to solve all of our problems when in actuality, the only one who can do that is God. Notice that the Psalmist doesn't just say that he will lie down and sleep, but that "in peace," he will lie down and sleep. His sleep was restful because he knew that God alone would keep him safe. We see this lived out when Jesus is asleep on the boat with the disciples during the storm. Only when we quit trying to control everything will we finally be able to find peaceful rest at night.

"Do not be anxious about anything, but in everything by prayer and supplication with thanksgiving let your request be made known to God. And the peace of God, which surpasses all understanding, will guard your hearts and your minds in Christ Jesus" (Philippians 4:6–7).

ABIDE IN LOVE

There is no fear in love. But perfect love drives
out fear, because fear has to do with punishment. The one who fears is not made perfect
in love. We love because He first loved us.
—1 John 4:18–19

Dr. Caroline Leaf said that the opposite of love is not hate, but fear. If we are honest with ourselves, much of what we do in life could be done out of a motivation of fear. We may work hard to get promoted at our jobs, because we are afraid of being a considered a failure; we may be kind to others only because we are afraid of being alone, or may even obey God only for what we can get out of it. If that's the case, then, we are only doing those things from a self-centered motivation, not love.

Our actions are based on fears of not getting something we desire, and those fears, while they may be helping us achieve something good, will become our master and enslave us. Perfect love, on the other hand, "drives out fear." When love becomes our motivation for working hard, serving others, or especially serving God, it is done from a selfless attitude that will free us from the binding emotion of fear. The only way we can begin to live out of a motivation of love is to understand that "He first loved us." God's love for us is unconditional in that "while we were sinners, Christ died for us." Let us break the chains of fear and step into the glorious light of God's love for us today.

"We please Him most, not by frantically trying to make ourselves good, but by throwing ourselves into His arms with all our imperfections and believing that He understands everything—and still loves us" (A. W. Tozer).

ABOVE AND BEYOND

> A man with leprosy came and knelt before
> him and said, "Lord, if you are willing, you
> can make me clean." Jesus reached out his
> hand and touched the man. "I am will-
> ing," he said. "Be clean!" Immediately,
> he was cleansed of his leprosy.
> —Matthew 8:2–3

Try to imagine for a moment what it would have been like to live with leprosy in Jesus's day. First of all, you had to sleep outside of the city. Then, during the day, if you were to come into town, you would have to shout, "Unclean, unclean," and stay at least twenty feet away from everyone. Most debilitating of all, you were not allowed to have physical contact with anyone because of the highly contagious nature of leprosy. You were completely shut off from society. You were considered unclean in every possible way. At the heart of it all, though, is the deep need rooted in every human being whom Tim Keller said is "to be known completely and loved unconditionally."

In this man's mind, in order to get that type of love, he must be healed physically. Jesus went far beyond this man's request. Notice that Jesus healed the man of his leprosy with His words, not His touch. But before He spoke physical healing, He touched the man. This was an enormous statement on the part of Jesus. He didn't have to do that. Jesus never does anything without a purpose behind it. What Jesus was essentially saying to the man was, "I am willing to give you your deepest need first. I love you in spite of your unclean-liness. As a matter of fact, the very thing you thought the physical healing would bring you, you already have in me and by the way, *I am willing.*" Just know that when we bring our request to God, He knows better than we do what we really need, and most important of all, He is willing.

"Now, to Him who is able to do infinitely more than all we ask or think, according to the power at work within us" (Ephesians 3:20).

INFINITE LOVE

"My son," the father said, "you are always
with me, and everything I have is yours.
But we had to celebrate and be glad,
because this brother of yours was dead and
is alive again; he was lost and is found."
—Luke 15:31–32

The parable of the prodigal son is perhaps the most well-known of all the parables told by Christ Jesus. It is a picture of a father with what seemingly appears to be an obedient son and a rebellious son. At first glance, the reader is moved by the father's love for the youngest son who squanders his inheritance on sinful living. But a closer look reveals that the father's love goes deeper than most people realize. His elder son reveals his real nature at the return of the younger. He responds to the father's order of a party with defiance by not entering. He then proceeds to tell the father all that he hasn't done for him over the years that he has "been slaving" for him. Imagine what the father in the story must be feeling watching this pitiful display of arrogance after the joyful return of his lost son.

Author and pastor, Tim Keller, points out something very important in regards to this scene in the story. He said that even after all of his son's disrespect, the father still invited his sons into the party. The father's love for us is infinite and unconditional. Praise God for His unfailing love.

"A person motivated by love rather than fear will not only obey the letter of the law, but will eagerly seek out new ways to carry out business with transparency and integrity" (Tim Keller).

No Greater Love

Greater love has no one than this, that someone lay down his life for his friends.

—John 15:13

Life can certainly have a way of beating us down to the point where
we question God's love. We ask ourselves, "Would a loving God
really allow me to go through this type of suffering and injustice?"
Answering the question of why we suffer is not easy, but the answer
to the question of "does God loves us?" is rather simple. All one has
to do to answer this question is look at the cross. Jesus endured an
enormous amount of suffering in order to restore us to His Father.
First of all, the sweating of blood in the garden caused His skin to be
more sensitive to pain. Then, the beating He endured while stand-
ing before the Jewish council. After that, He was scourged by the
Romans nearly to death. This alone caused Him to not even look
human on the cross, not to mention almost killed Him. Next, the
crown of thorns which were beaten onto His head with sticks. Then,
next event was His painful walk down the Via Dolorosa while carry-
ing His cross. Finally, at Golgotha, He was pierced for our iniquities
by the nails in His hands and feet. All of this paled in comparison
to the suffering He would endure spiritually. And to think, Christ
did all this so that I may spend eternity in fellowship with Him, the
Father, and the Holy Spirit. Does God love us? Look at the cross.

"God proved His love on the Cross. When Christ hung, and bled,
and died, it was God saying to the world, I love you" (Billy Graham).

WITH THE JOY SET BEFORE HIM

Looking to Jesus, the founder and perfecter of
our faith, *who for the joy that was set before him
endured the cross*, despising the shame, and is
seated at the right hand of the throne of God.
—Hebrews 12:2

We always think about the suffering that Christ endured before and during
the cross. What we tend to forget is this passage in Hebrews 12:2 when it
says, "Who for the joy that was set before him endured the cross." What a
powerful statement! He had a joy set before Him? What was that joy? The
joy set before Jesus was that of our future with Him in heaven. He never
lost sight of why He went to the cross. To know that Christ was looking
forward and was excited about our coming home someday while on His
way to His crucifixion, should stir our hearts as believers. Jesus is eager for
the wedding ceremony that will someday take place between Himself and
His bride, the church. When learning to abide in love, it would bless us
to remember that Jesus had us as His joy which helped Him endure the
Cross. Someday for us, that joy will be complete. Let us praise God all of
our days until we have the joy of seeing our Groom face-to-face.

When will all get to heaven
What a day of rejoicing that will be
When we all see Jesus
We'll sing and shout the victory
When We All Get to Heaven
Eliza Edmunds Hewitt

ABOUT THE AUTHOR

Clay Meadows was born in Columbus, Georgia, in May of 1981. In 2008, he began teaching Bible at a Christian school in Memphis, Tennessee, where he graduated as a student. In the last eleven years, Clay has continued teaching the Word of God to the next generation along with taking on the role as junior high counselor.

Clay received his master's degree in Christian studies from Union University in 2017. After Clay began teaching Bible, he quickly realized his passion and calling in teaching Christ to others. He would later form a mentoring group with the help of other male faculty and staff for junior high boys in teaching them what it means to be a man of God. Clay's passion for Christ began in his home growing up. His father and mother showed him a genuine love for Jesus and lived in such a way that was honoring to God. As Clay grew older, he would routinely talk with his father in depth about the Lord. Clay's father, who has been leading Christian schools for over forty years as a head of school, has had the greatest impact on the person Clay has become today. Clay will readily admit that the influence of his earthly father has led him to have deep relationship with his Heavenly Father.

Clay Meadows currently lives in Memphis, Tennessee, with his wife and two children.